Desmond at the Carnival

by Althea
illustrated by the author

© 1981 Rourke Publications, Inc.
© 1978 Althea Braithwaite
 first published by Dinosaur
 Publications Limited, England

Published by Rourke Publications, Inc., P.O. Box 868, Windermere, Florida 32786. Copyright © 1981 by Rourke Publications, Inc. All copyrights reserved. No part of this book may be reproduced in any form without written permission from the publisher. Printed in the United States of America.

Library of Congress Cataloging in Publication Data

Althea.
 Desmond at the carnival.

 SUMMARY: Desmond helps round up two escaped carnival lions.
 [1. Lions—Fiction. 2. Dinosaurs—Fiction]
 I. Title.
PZ7.A4638Dd [E] 80-39745
ISBN 0-86625-102-2

Rourke Publications, Inc.
Windermere, Florida

Desmond was in his garden.
He was looking at the flowers.
Mr. Jones, who lived next door,
looked over the fence.

"Hello Desmond. Are you coming
to the carnival tomorrow?" he said.

"Oh! A carnival!" said Desmond.
"That is exciting. May I come with you?"

Desmond had never been to a carnival.
He did not really know
what he was going to see.

The next morning, they walked to the town square.

There were lots of merry-go-rounds, and a ferris wheel.

"I think I will ride
on the ferris wheel," said Desmond.

"I am sorry, you cannot ride
on my ferris wheel.
You are much too big,"
said the man.

Poor Desmond was too big
to fit on any of the rides.
He felt very sad.

There were monkeys and bears,
and kangaroos and zebras.

Mr. Jones was giving an apple
to one of the elephants.
Some people came running by.

They looked very frightened.

"What is the matter?" asked Desmond.

"The lions have escaped!" they shouted and they ran away.

"Dear me," said Desmond.
"I had better go see what can be done!"

He hurried along. Suddenly, he came face to face with two big lions. They were growling!

"Hello," said Desmond,
in a nervous voice.
"What is the matter?"

"Nobody gave us lunch today.
We are very hungry,"
said the lions, together.

"Oh dear," said Desmond.
"You poor things.
Let us try to find the zoo keeper.
We will tell him."

The lions went with Desmond
to search for the zoo keeper.

When they found him, Desmond said,
"These lions have not had any lunch,
Mr. Zoo Keeper."

"Gosh!" said the keeper.
"I was so busy I forgot to feed them.
How very silly of me.
I will go and get their food right away."

The lions went back into their cage.
Desmond talked to them
while the keeper went
to get their meal.

The lions finished eating their meat. Then,
Mr. Jones bought three strawberry ice cream cones.
They were a special treat for Desmond
and the two lions.

In the afternoon, there was a parade.
The lions asked Desmond
if he would walk with them
through the streets.

Everyone cheered as they went by.
People will talk about the carnival
for a long time afterwards.

And, the zoo keeper never again forgot to feed the lions.